EXECUTIVE OFFICE OF THE PRESIDENT
NATIONAL SCIENCE AND TECHNOLOGY COUNCIL
WASHINGTON, D.C. 20502

March 23, 2016

Dear Stakeholder:

The United States Government invests in Earth observations that are critical to the protection of lives and property, national security, economic growth, and scientific inquiry. These data provide the fundamental basis for our understanding of all Earth-system phenomena, including weather and climate, natural hazards, land-use change, ecosystem health, and natural-resource availability.

A core principle of the U.S. Government is that Federal Earth-observation data are public goods, paid for by the American people, and that free, full, and open access to these data significantly enhances their value. The return on our annual Earth-observation investment increases in accordance with the data's widespread use in public- and private-sector decision-making.

Through the advocacy of the international Group on Earth Observations and the leadership of the United States, international data sharing has increased dramatically over the past decade. Our international engagement provides U.S. entities with access to valuable new sources of Earth-observation data.

The success of all of these activities rests on effective Federal data-management practices, at a time when increasing data volumes introduce new management challenges. The interagency *Common Framework for Earth Observation Data* represents a collective step forward toward addressing these challenges, by improving the discoverability, accessibility, and usability of Earth-observation data.

The Framework was developed by OSTP through an interagency effort led by the Data Management Working Group of the U.S. Group on Earth Observations, a subcommittee of the National Science and Technology Council's Committee on Environment, Natural Resources, and Sustainability. The Framework is intended to assist the data-management community in making decisions that will facilitate the greatest benefit to the United States and international community from our vast collective investment in Earth observations.

I expect the guidelines in this document to serve the United States and global community well in more effectively managing Earth-system data for societal benefit.

Sincerely,

Tamara L. Dickinson
Principal Assistant Director for Environment and Energy and
Co-Chair, Committee on Environment, Sustainability, and Natural Resources
National Science and Technology Council
Office of Science and Technology Policy

About the National Science and Technology Council

The National Science and Technology Council (NSTC) is the principal means by which the Executive Branch coordinates science and technology policy across the diverse entities that make up the Federal research and development (R&D) enterprise. One of the NSTC's primary objectives is establishing clear national goals for Federal science and technology investments. The NSTC prepares R&D packages aimed at accomplishing multiple national goals. The NSTC's work is organized under five committees: Environment, Natural Resources, and Sustainability; Homeland and National Security; Science, Technology, Engineering, and Mathematics (STEM) Education; Science; and Technology. Each of these committees oversees subcommittees and working groups that are focused on different aspects of science and technology. More information is available at www.whitehouse.gov/ostp/nstc.

About the White House Office of Science and Technology Policy

The White House Office of Science and Technology Policy (OSTP) was established by the National Science and Technology Policy, Organization, and Priorities Act of 1976. OSTP's responsibilities include advising the President in policy formulation and budget development on questions in which science and technology are important elements; articulating the President's science and technology policy and programs; and fostering strong partnerships among Federal, state, and local governments, and the scientific communities in industry and academia. The Director of OSTP also serves as Assistant to the President for Science and Technology and manages the NSTC. More information is available at http://www.whitehouse.gov/ostp.

About the U.S. Group on Earth Observations Subcommittee

The United States Group on Earth Observations (USGEO) is chartered as a subcommittee of the NSTC Committee on Environment, Natural Resources, and Sustainability (CENRS). The Subcommittee's purpose is threefold: to coordinate, plan, and assess Federal Earth observation activities in cooperation with domestic stakeholders; to foster improved Earth system data management and interoperability throughout the Federal Government; and to engage international stakeholders by formulating the U.S. position for, and coordinating U.S. participation in the intergovernmental Group on Earth Observations. More information is available at http://www.usgeo.gov.

About the Data Management Working Group

The Data Management Working Group (DMWG) is chartered by and reports to USGEO. DMWG members, who are representatives of the various agencies within USGEO, developed this Common Framework document. The DMWG's charter calls for the group to foster "the implementation of an interagency framework for life-cycle data management, stewardship and preservation for Earth-observation data." The scope of work within its jurisdiction includes "...data-management principles, approaches, data architecture considerations, data standardization, and data access and sharing policies..." The overall DMWG purpose is strengthening interagency access and sharing of Earth-observation data in order to extend and maximize agency investments made in data management and stewardship.

About this Document

This document was developed by the Data Management Working Group of USGEO. The USGEO Plan of Work for 2014–2016 includes as a priority action: "Establish criteria for assessing the relative capabilities in discoverability, accessibility, and usability of Earth observations data." This document was completed as the result of that action. It was reviewed by the USGEO Subcommittee and CENRS and was finalized and published by OSTP.

Acknowledgements

OSTP and the DMWG would like to acknowledge the contributions of Timothy Stryker, Director of the USGEO Program; Reid Sherman, American Association for the Advancement of Science Fellow at the National Aeronautics and Space Administration; and Jason Gallo and Emily Nightingale of the IDA Science and Technology Policy Institute in the development of this document.

Copyright Information

Report prepared by

NATIONAL SCIENCE AND TECHNOLOGY COUNCIL
COMMITTEE ON ENVIRONMENT, NATURAL RESOURCES, AND SUSTAINABILITY
U.S. GROUP ON EARTH OBSERVATIONS SUBCOMMITTEE
DATA MANAGEMENT WORKING GROUP

National Science and Technology Council

Chair
John P. Holdren
Assistant to the President for Science
and Technology and Director,
White House Office of Science and Technology
Policy

Staff
Afua Bruce
Executive Director

Committee on Environment, Natural Resources, and Sustainability

Chairs
Tamara Dickinson
White House Office of Science and Technology
Policy

Thomas Burke
Environmental Protection Agency

Kathleen Sullivan
Department of Commerce,
National Oceanic and Atmospheric
Administration

Executive Secretary
Lisa Matthews
Environmental Protection Agency

U.S. Group on Earth Observations Subcommittee

Chair
David Hermreck
White House Office of Science and Technology
Policy

Vice Chairs
Lawrence Friedl
National Aeronautics and Space Administration

Tim Newman
Department of the Interior,
U.S. Geological Survey

Zdenka Willis
Department of Commerce,
National Oceanic and Atmospheric
Administration

Data Management Working Group

Chairs

Jeff de La Beaujardiere
Department of Commerce,
National Oceanic and Atmospheric
Administration

Mike Frame
Department of Interior,
U.S. Geological Survey

Jeff Walter
National Aeronautics and Space Administration

Members

Thomas Adang	Department of Defense, Office of the Secretary of Defense
James Bailey	Department of Defense, National Geospatial-Intelligence Agency
Michael Bosilovich	National Aeronautics and Space Administration
Sky Bristol	Department of the Interior, U.S. Geological Survey
Ken Casey	Department of Commerce, National Oceanic and Atmospheric Administration
Rich Frazier	Department of the Interior, U.S. Geological Survey
Amy Friedlander	National Science Foundation
Justin "Jay" Hnilo	Department of Energy
Vivian Hutchison	Department of the Interior, U.S. Geological Survey
Ed Kearns	Department of Commerce, National Oceanic and Atmospheric Administration
Kevin Kirby	Environmental Protection Agency
Bradley Mabe	Department of Commerce, National Oceanic and Atmospheric Administration
Dave Meyer	National Aeronautics and Space Administration
Kevin Murphy	National Aeronautics and Space Administration
Steve Newman	Department of Defense, U.S. Army
Ted Payne	U.S. Department of Agriculture
Barbara Ransom	National Science Foundation
Derrick Snowden	Department of Commerce, National Oceanic and Atmospheric Administration
William Sonntag	Environmental Protection Agency
Thornton Staples	Smithsonian Institution
Curt Tilmes	National Aeronautics and Space Administration
Amy Walton	National Science Foundation
Elizabeth Warner	Department of Defense, U.S. Navy
Eric Wise	Department of Defense, U.S. Air Force
Robert Wolfe	U.S. Global Change Research Program

Table of Contents

Executive Summary

Globally, billions of dollars are invested annually in Earth observations that support public services, commercial activity, and scientific inquiry. Each year, the member agencies of the U.S. Group on Earth Observations (USGEO) invest more than $4 billion dollars in civil Earth observations. Through these investments, the U.S. Government ensures that the Nation's decision makers, emergency responders, scientists, business owners, farmers, and a wide array of other stakeholders have the information they need about climate and weather, disaster events, land-use change, ecosystem health, natural resources, and many other characteristics of the Earth system. Taken together, Earth observations provide an indispensable foundation for advancing and sustaining the economic, environmental, and social well-being of the United States.

While Federally-managed Earth observations are typically collected for a specific purpose, these data are often found to be useful in other applications, including use by state, local, and international decision-makers and in the private sector. It is therefore essential to manage and preserve observations data so that users can find, evaluate, understand, and utilize them in new and unanticipated ways. The wide range of scientific and observation efforts across the Federal agencies, and the diverse types of data collected as a result, require a data-management approach that can be both applied broadly and tailored to particular needs.

The Common Framework for Earth Observations Data provides guidance to data producers in Federal agencies for improving and standardizing their data-management practices. This document is primarily concerned with data from the Federal Government's Earth-observing systems, though its recommendations may be useful for others, such as local, state, international, and commercial data creators whose Earth observations are widely shared.

The recommendations in the Common Framework are focused on the discoverability, accessibility, and usability of Earth observations and derived data products Topics addressed include Data-Search and Discovery Services, Data-Access Services, Data Documentation, and a section on Compatible Formats and Vocabularies.

The recommendations in this document are not requirements, but can serve as a reference for data managers and users on a suggested subset of the many available standards. The recommendations in this document are intended to be broadly applicable, but not comprehensive. There may be types of observations and special cases for which other practices will be necessary. Where the recommendations fit the circumstances, their application will help ensure that Earth-observation data are more discoverable, accessible, and usable.

1. Background

1.1 Purpose of the Common Framework

Each year, member agencies of the U.S. Group on Earth Observations (USGEO) invest more than $4 billion dollars in civil Earth observations. Through these investments, the U.S. Government ensures that the Nation's decision makers, emergency responders, scientists, business owners, farmers, and a wide array of other stakeholders have the information they need about climate and weather, disaster events, land-use change, ecosystem health, natural resources, and many other characteristics of the Earth system. Taken together, Earth observations provide an indispensable foundation for advancing and sustaining the economic, environmental, and social well-being of the United States.

While Federally managed Earth observations are typically collected for a specific purpose, these data are often found to be useful in other applications. It is therefore essential to manage and preserve observations data so that users can find, evaluate, understand, and utilize them in new and unanticipated ways. The wide range of scientific and observation efforts across the Federal agencies, and the diverse types of data collected as a result, require a data-management approach that can be both applied broadly and tailored to particular needs.

The U.S. Government is committed to making Federal civil Earth-observation data freely available to all users. Even without financial barriers, technical impediments to using these data to their full potential often exist. To enhance the discoverability, accessibility, and usability of Earth-observation data, the Common Framework for Earth-Observation Data (referred to in this document as the "Common Framework") provides Federal agencies with a recommended set of standards and practices to follow as they develop new observing systems or modernize existing data collections. By standardizing the protocols for finding, accessing, and using Earth-observation data, the Common Framework will make it easier to obtain and assemble data from diverse sources for improved analysis, understanding, decision-making, community resilience, and commercial use.

The standards recommended in this document are not new. In fact, many of the standards for data access and documentation are existing standards that have been endorsed by the Federal Geographic Data Committee (FGDC),[1] an interagency committee within the U.S. Government that promotes the national coordinated development, use, sharing, and dissemination of geospatial data. All the standards recommended are also found in the Global Earth Observation System of Systems (GEOSS) Standards and Interoperability Registry.[2] What is new about the Common Framework is the recommendation to use a focused subset of the standards of that list to increase data interoperability among Federal agencies (see Figure 1 for a representation of this conceptual model). In addition, the Common Framework provides detail on how best to implement the standards.

---

[1] The full list of FGDC Endorsed Standards can be found at http://www.fgdc.gov/standards/fgdc-endorsed-external-standards.

[2] The GEOSS Standards and Interoperability Registry can be found at http://seabass.ieee.org/groups/geoss/index.php.

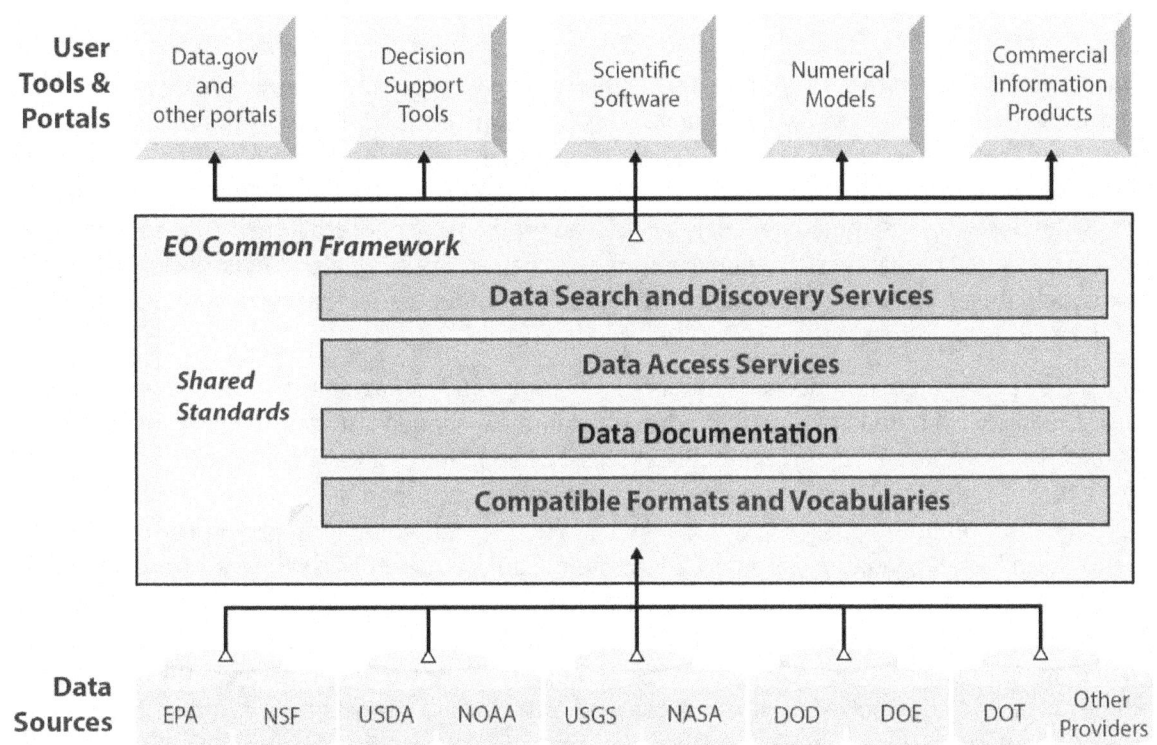

Notes: This is a conceptual model of the Common Framework for Earth-Observation Data. Examples of Federal agencies (and other data providers) are represented at the bottom of the diagram as sources of Earth-observation data. User tools and catalogs, shown along the top, include the portals (such as http://data.gov and other thematic or agency-specific portals) that enable users to search for data and the software applications that can read the data and enable users to view and analyze data for decision support, scientific discovery, numerical modeling, and creation of new, value-added information products based on the observations. The Common Framework, shown in the center, seeks to simplify the discovery, access, and use of the data by recommending specific standards for exchanging information between data sources and user tools. The recommendations focus on computer-to-computer data exchange and are therefore intended primarily for developers of software that produce, distribute, read, or find the data. Example data sources shown are the Environmental Protection Agency (EPA), National Science Foundation (NSF), U.S. Department of Agriculture (USDA), National Oceanic and Atmospheric Administration (NOAA), U.S. Geological Survey (USGS), National Aeronautics and Space Administration (NASA), Department of Defense (DOD), Department of Energy (DOE), and Department of Transportation (DOT).

Figure 1. Conceptual model of the Common Framework for Earth-Observation Data

1.2 Target Audience of the Common Framework

The primary intent of the Common Framework is to provide guidance to data producers in Federal agencies for improving and standardizing their data-management practices. Therefore, this document addresses data from the Federal Government's civil Earth-observing systems. Additionally, the White House Office of Science and Technology Policy (OSTP) recommends that Federal agencies that provide extramural funding for the collection of Earth-observation data by external partners include these data-management recommendations in grant and contract language. This document also informs data users, software and tool developers, and information-product producers about which standards are preferred by USGEO agencies. This information can assist them in harmonizing their activities with current Federal data-management practices. These recommendations may also be useful for local, state, international, and commercial data creators whose Earth observations are widely shared.

1.3 Scope of the Common Framework

The recommendations in this document are focused on the discoverability, accessibility and usability of Earth observations and derived data products.[3] The Common Framework adopts the definition of Earth-observation data used by the 2013 *National Strategy for Civil Earth Observations*. We use the terms "data" and "Earth observations" interchangeably to mean geo-referenced digital information about Earth, including the observations, metadata, imagery, derived products, and forecasts and analyses produced by computer models. Non-digital data, published papers, data-processing algorithms (including computer source code), preserved geological or biological samples, or other media that have not been digitized are not in the scope of this document.

This document originated as a mechanism for coordinating data-management improvements carried out through the Big Earth Data Initiative (BEDI, described in the Appendix). It was originally intended to give clear guidance to agencies on which practices to use when managing data under the auspices of BEDI. Because the recommendations had considerable interagency support and may be applicable to data management at Federal agencies more broadly, OSTP decided to release the Common Framework publicly. These recommendations are not requirements, but can serve as a reference for data managers and users on a suggested subset of the many available standards. The goal of the Common Framework is to narrow the scope of what is permissible for BEDI-funded projects, and to recommend that others adopt the same standards in order to maximize interoperability. The recommendations in this document are intended to be broadly applicable, but not comprehensive. Data-processing algorithms and computer source code are not in the scope of this document, though for scientific reproducibility it is beneficial to make such code publicly accessible. Non-digital data, published papers, preserved geological or biological samples, or other media that have not been digitized are also not in scope.

1.4 Version Control in the Common Framework

Many of the standards and protocols recommended in the Common Framework go through multiple versions and continuing development. The recommendations in this document are intended to not be so specific that they soon will be out of date. Nevertheless, newer standards will be developed and different practices and protocols will eventually come to be widespread and appropriate. The Common Framework is intended to be adapted as necessary. The principles and philosophy will stay in place, but the specific practices recommended will be reviewed periodically by the USGEO Data Management Working Group (DMWG) to ensure that the guidance in the Common Framework is reasonably current.

1.5 Structure of the Common Framework

The following aspects of data management are considered in this document:

- Data Search and Discovery Services
- Data-Access Services
- Data Documentation
- Compatible Formats and Vocabularies

Within the sections about each aspect, the recommended best practices are described at three or more levels, to include:

---

[3] This document does not provide guidance on quality assurance and user feedback mechanisms for Earth-observation data.

- *Standards and Protocols*—officially endorsed standards for use in Earth-observation data management.

- *Methods and Practices*—recommended ways to use the endorsed standards, including making data open by default per Project Open Data guidelines announced by Office of Management and Budget (OMB) Memorandum M-13-13.

- *Implementations*—available software to use in realizing the standards and examples of use of the standards at Federal agencies. These are not endorsements but are pointers for users of this document to find more information.

This document makes use of numerous acronyms and abbreviations. Frequently-occurring acronyms and abbreviations are listed in the Appendix.

2. Data Search and Discovery Services

2.1 Introduction

Searching for relevant data is often the first step in addressing a new problem or research question. Federal agencies should seek to ensure that Earth observations are readily discoverable by the diverse community of domestic and international information providers and users. Data collected for a particular purpose can only be reused for novel purposes if those unanticipated users know the data exists, and are able to find it, assess its utility, and understand how it was generated. This section provides guidance on the creation and organization of searchable catalogs of data, which are created by harvesting metadata, both "structural" (defined as information about the containers of data) and "descriptive" (defined as instances of data content or its use), formatted in a standardized manner. In particular, these standards will assist agencies in ensuring their data are discoverable on data.gov, as required by OMB M-13-13.

Typically, an organization will establish an online page or portal with a human-oriented user interface to allow individuals to find data. This is a useful first step, but it is by no means sufficient—modern catalogs also need to be searchable by automated software including search engines, other catalogs, and decision-support software. These catalogs need enable users to run various kinds of searches and retrieve metadata records or summarization of metadata in the results. Accordingly, the *National Strategy for Civil Earth Observations* called for the establishment of formal, standards-based catalog services that would enable commercial search engines to index data holdings.

The standards below, properly applied, can be used to meet the following Data-Management Principles (DMPs) from the international Group on Earth Observations (GEO) Strategic Plan (see Appendix):

- **DMP-1**: Data and all associated metadata will be discoverable through catalogs and search engines, and data access and use conditions, including licenses, will be clearly indicated.

- **DMP-10**: Data will be assigned appropriate persistent, resolvable identifiers to enable documents to cite the data on which they are based, and to enable data providers to receive acknowledgement of use of their data.

2.2 Standards and Protocols

For many users, the search for information begins with a commercial search engine that crawls the entire indexed Web. Search engines typically work by indexing the text on a page, so they cannot detect that a page is about Earth-observation data without appropriate text identifiers. Therefore, the Common Framework recommends:

- Generating metadata required by Project Open Data (https://project-open-data.cio.gov), which employs schema.org vocabularies (https://schema.org) tags for data-set landing pages. Schema.org creates, maintains, and promotes schemas for structured data on the Internet. These tags can convey information such as: geographic coverage (https://schema.org/GeoCoordinates), temporal coverage (https://schema.org/datasetTimeInterval), and other dataset attributes (https://schema.org/Dataset).

While many users will utilize external search engines for search and discovery, many others will begin their search in published catalogs. Thus, as appropriate and as driven by user demand, data providers should create their own searchable catalogs as well as contribute open data records to external search engines. To improve discoverability and simplify metadata management, individual observations from a single observing system that collects data at multiple times or locations should be aggregated into larger groupings, and users should be able to search and filter based on temporal and geographic attributes.

For instance, all Federal agencies, per OMB memorandum M-13-13[4] with the subject "Open Data Policy – Managing Information as an Asset" are required to collect or create information in a way that supports downstream information-processing and dissemination activities. As part of this memorandum, Federal agencies are required to create catalogs of their data inventories.

One or both of the following Application Programming Interfaces (APIs) is recommended to allow computer programs to search catalogs:

- Open Geospatial Consortium (OGC, http://www.opengeospatial.org/) Easy Catalog Services for the Web (CSW, http://www.ogcnetwork.net/node/630) includes interface standards that specify the interfaces, bindings, and framework for defining application profiles required to publish and access digital catalogs of metadata for geospatial data, services, and related resources. CSW is specifically designed for searching geographic data. It allows searches to specify locations and time periods of interest, and it supports the metadata standard recommended in the Data Documentation section.

- OpenSearch (http://www.opensearch.org/) is a collection of simple formats for sharing search results that are generically applicable to any type of data. OpenSearch extensions to support geographic or temporal queries are currently in draft form. Geo and Time extensions for OpenSearch are specified by OGC (http://www.opengeospatial.org/standards/opensearchgeo) to provide spatial and temporal queries to a repository of geospatial content.

To allow the combination of project- or organization-specific catalogs into more-general catalogs by harvesting metadata, the Common Framework recommends:

- Open Archives Initiative—Protocol for Metadata Harvesting (OAI-PMH, https://www.openarchives.org/pmh/) is a low-barrier mechanism for repository interoperability that allows a catalog to harvest all or part of the metadata from another catalog. The harvest can include only recent changes to data or only particular collections of data.

To enable specific datasets to be cited in journal articles, documents, webpages, or workflow descriptions, the Common Framework recommends:

- Digital Object Identifiers (DOIs), such as DataCite or others, be assigned to datasets. DataCite (https://www.datacite.org/) assigns persistent identifiers to datasets to increase data accessibility. A DOI is equivalent to a serial number for a dataset; once assigned, the DOI stays the same even if data are moved to another Web site or organization. DOIs should be assigned at a fairly coarse level of granularity (for example, one DOI for an entire time-series of data, rather than separate DOIs for every measurement).

2.3 Methods and Practices

The following suggested methods or practices can supplement the recommendations above.

---

[4] see https://www.whitehouse.gov/sites/default/files/omb/memoranda/2013/m-13-13.pdf

Catalog registration method:

- Provide the Uniform Resource Locator (URL) of the Web Accessible Folder (WAF) containing International Organization for Standardization (ISO) metadata to agency-specific catalogs (e.g., data.doi.gov, data.doe.gov), data.gov, Geoplatform.gov, or to other catalogs as appropriate, as described in the Data Documentation section.

- Legacy data using FGDC Content Standard for Digital Geospatial Metadata (CSDGM) is accepted for legacy datasets that cannot comply with newly defined and adopted standards.

Persistent Identifier Use:

- When possible, values for metadata fields should also include persistent, resolvable identifiers. For example, when a person's name is given, if that person has an existing persistent identifier, then that identifier, along with the establishing authority, should also be provided.

2.4 Implementations

Several example implementations and the supporting standards are described below.

2.4.1 Software Available to Help Implement Standards

Several types of open-source and commercial off-the-shelf (COTS) software exist that support the recommended standards, including:

- Comprehensive Kerbal Archive Network (CKAN) (http://ckan.org/) is open source software.

- Geoportal Server (https://github.com/Esri/geoportal-server/) is open-source software.

- Geonetwork (http://geonetwork-opensource.org/) is open-source software.

- GeoTools (http://www.geotools.org/) is an open-source toolkit that implements OGC-CSW and other OGC protocols.

2.4.2 Examples of Implementation

Examples of organizations that have implemented systems utilizing the recommended standards are:

- National Oceanic and Atmospheric Administration (NOAA) Data Catalog (https://data.noaa.gov/) uses CKAN.

- The National Aeronautics and Space Administration (NASA) Earth Observing System (EOS) Clearing House (ECHO, https://earthdata.nasa.gov/echo) is open-source.

- U.S. Geological Survey (USGS) ScienceBase (http://www.sciencebase.gov/) uses GeoTools and the USGS Science Data Catalog (data.usgs.gov) uses various open-source components.

- OpenTopography (http://www.opentopography.org/) is supported by USGS and NSF to facilitate access to Earth-science topography data and tools, and to assign DOIs to all datasets.

2.5 Testing and Validation

The adoption and incorporation of various testing and validation methodologies is critical to system performance and interoperability. Additional information is contained below.

- Unit tests (e.g., catalog responds with correct number of records for query; information from each record is correct).

- Interoperability tests (e.g., catalog client is successfully able to communicate with catalog server; metadata harvest or distributed search works correctly).

- Scenario-based tests (e.g., ability to find relevant data to address particular scenario).

  o U.S. Integrated Ocean Observing System (IOOS®, github.com/ioos/system-test) uses scenario-based tests.

2.6 Metrics

The following metrics will be measured by automatically gathering statistical information from authoritative data catalogs (e.g., data.gov, Geoplatform.gov):

- Number of datasets listed in each catalog.

- Number of datasets that meet the U.S. Chief Information Officer qualifications for open data: publicly accessible under an open license with no restrictions on reuse. See the full Open Data Principles at https://project-open-data.cio.gov/principles.

- Percentage of USGEO Earth Observations Assessment (EOA) Observing Systems listed in one of the Agency data catalogs.

- Percentage of datasets in catalog with one or more of the Common Framework data-access methods offered.

3. Data-Access Services

3.1 Introduction

Data-access services focus on the ways that users retrieve data for exploration, analysis, and decision-making. In the past, users might have been limited to downloading an entire dataset, or data providers might have required the use of project-specific portals or Web applications as the sole method for data access. The Common Framework encourages data providers to offer services and application programming interfaces (APIs) that provide more-advanced access to datasets, such as subsetting, aggregation, or visualization. These methods return data more relevant to the user's specific problem. An additional benefit is that as more data providers offer the same standards-based services, it becomes easier to obtain and combine data from multiple sources without additional programming or post-processing. The goal is to move closer to simple, universal access to all Federal Earth observations as a common service, independent of lower-level technical details of data-access mechanisms.

The standards and protocols described below support the following DMP from the GEO Strategic Plan:

- **DMP-2**: Data will be accessible via online services, including, at minimum, direct download, but preferably user-customizable services for visualization and computation.

3.2 Standards and Protocols

Many Earth observations are "georeferenced," meaning that the location on Earth of the observation is described by Earth-based coordinates such as latitude and longitude, as opposed to a street address or political boundaries.[5] "Raster images" are images that are structured as pixel-by-pixel data, as opposed to a set of line segments and shapes. The recommended data-access services for map-based visualizations of georeferenced data, or direct access to raster imagery are:

- OGC Web Map Service (WMS, http://www.opengeospatial.org/standards/wms) provides a simple Hypertext Transfer Protocol (HTTP) interface for requesting geo-registered map images from one or more distributed geospatial databases.

- OGC Web Map Tile Service (WMTS, http://www.opengeospatial.org/standards/wmts) protocol serves map tiles of spatially referenced data using tile images with predefined content, extent, and resolution.

When data are accessed in numerical rather than image form, they are often structured into a grid by location, especially for remote-sensing data. For regularly gridded data, where the elements within the grid are the same size, the recommendation is:

---

[5] In addition, many coordinate projections are possible and should be referenced or associated with each dataset so that translation tools may convert among the different Earth geometries to compare maps on an equal basis. Popular Earth projections include: Azimuthal Equidistant (AED) (azimuth lines are straight and angles not distorted), Mercator (lines of latitude and longitude are straight and intersect in right angles), Polar Stereographic (AED at the north pole), Universal Transverse Mercator (UTM, axis reverses at a select longitude with horizontal dimension compressed), Perspective (satellite view), Equidistant Cylinder (used in digital terrain maps), Gnomonic (all great circle arcs are straight lines), Gauss Conformal (UTM minus the horizontal compression), Lambert Conformal Conic (scale is true along two standard parallels, used in aeronautical charts), and Lambert Azimuthal Equal-Area (straight line distance from center point equals straight in 3D distance through the globe).

- Open-source Project for a Network Data Access Protocol (OPeNDAP, http://www.opendap.org/support) is a data-transmission protocol designed specifically for science data. Also see https://earthdata.nasa.gov/standards/data-access-protocol-2.

- OGC Web Coverage Service (WCS, http://www.opengeospatial.org/standards/wcs) provides multi-dimensional coverage data for access over the Internet.

Sometimes data are in an unstructured grid, meaning that elements cannot be described by a simple set of coordinates because they are not of uniform size. For data in such a form, the recommendation is:

- Unstructured Grid (UGRID, https://github.com/ugrid-conventions/ugrid-conventions/blob/v0.9.0/ugrid-conventions.md) provides metadata conventions for scientific data using unstructured grids.

For *in situ* data, meaning data taken at the location of observation by one or more stationary or moving sensors:

- OGC Sensor Observation Service (SOS, http://www.opengeospatial.org/standards/sos) defines a web-service interface that allows querying observations, sensor metadata, and representations of observed features for managing data in an interoperable way.

- OGC Web Feature Service (WFS, http://www.opengeospatial.org/standards/wfs) allows users to retrieve or modify specific data relevant to the user.

- Data Access Protocol (DAP) with discrete sampling geometries (https://www.nodc.noaa.gov/data/formats/netcdf/).

For data that is not geo-referenced, but is described by geographic features such as political boundaries, roads, etc.:

- OGC WFS (as noted above).

For tabular data, meaning data structured in tables (e.g., where each column is a different piece of information) rather than grids:

- TableDAP (http://coastwatch.pfeg.noaa.gov/erddap/tabledap/) allows the use of the OPeNDAP constraint/selection protocol to request data subsets, graphs, and maps from tabular datasets.

3.3 Methods and Practices

The following suggested methods or practices can supplement the recommendations above.

- Adopt the WMS 1.3 Best Practice for Time and Elevation issued by the OGC Meteorology/Oceanography Domain Working Group (https://portal.opengeospatial.org/files/?artifact_id=56394).

- If using commercial software that offers both proprietary services and open standards services, turn on options for standard services. For instance, Esri's ArcGIS Server platform has options for turning on OGC capabilities to provide WMS, WFS, or WCS in addition to Esri proprietary services, but these capabilities are not generally turned on by default.

- Large-file download remains an issue when using HTTP, and success depends on many networking factors. Where possible, employ bit-streaming protocols or file-subsetting capabilities to mitigate this issue.

3.4 Implementations

Several example implementations and the supporting standards are described below.

3.4.1 Software Available to Implement Standards

The following software can be used to implement these services. Inclusion on this list does not constitute formal endorsement by the U.S. Government; no warranty regarding suitability, security, or performance of software is expressed or implied.

- DAP:
  - Thematic Real-Time Environmental Distributed Data Services (THREDDS) Data Server (http://www.unidata.ucar.edu/software/thredds/current/tds/) is free, open-source software.
  - Hyrax Data Server (http://www.opendap.org/download/hyrax) is free, open-source software.
  - NOAA Environmental Research Division's Data Access Program (ERDDAP) (http://coastwatch.pfeg.noaa.gov/erddap/) is free, open-source software.

- WMS:
  - MapServer (http://mapserver.org/) is free, open-source software.
  - NOAA ERDDAP (http://coastwatch.pfeg.noaa.gov/erddap/) is free, open-source software.
  - Geoserver (http://geoserver.org/) is free, open-source software.
  - Boundless OpenGeo Suite (http://boundlessgeo.com/solutions/opengeo-suite/) is not free and includes GeoServer and other components, which are built on open-source software.
  - Sci-WMS (https://github.com/asascience-open/sci-wms) is a Python WMS for unstructured grid data distributed via OPeNDAP and is open-source software.
  - ncWMS (http://www.opengeospatial.org/standards/wms) is a WMS for geospatial data that are stored in Network Common Data Form (NetCDF, http://www.unidata.ucar.edu/software/netcdf/) files that are compliant with Climate and Forecast (CF) conventions (http://www.cfconventions.org/). ncWMS is open-source software that can be deployed as a stand-alone application or as a plugin for a THREDDS Data Server (http://www.resc.rdg.ac.uk/trac/ncWMS/).
  - Esri's ArcGIS Server with OGC option enabled is a geographic information system (GIS) and is not free.

- SOS:
  - U.S. IOOS® customized build of the 52°North Sensor Observation Service (SOS Project page: http://ioos.github.io/i52n-sos/; GitHub Repository: https://github.com/ioos/i52n-sos) is free, open-source software.
  - ncSOS plugin for the THREDDS Data Server (https://github.com/asascience-open/ncSOS) is free, open-source software.

- TableDAP:
  - NOAA ERDDAP (http://coastwatch.pfeg.noaa.gov/erddap/) is free, open-source software.

3.4.2 Examples of Implementation

The following are instances of Federal use of these data-access services.

- DAP:
  - NOAA Operational Model Archive and Distribution System (NOMADS, http://nomads.ncdc.noaa.gov/) is open-source software.
  - NOAA Unified Access Framework (UAF, https://geo-ide.noaa.gov/) is open-source software.
  - USGS ScienceBase (https://www.sciencebase.gov/catalog/) is a dynamic query returning data assets with OPeNDAP end points.
- WMS:
  - NOAA nowCoast (http://nowcoast.noaa.gov/help/mapservices.shtml?name=mapservices) is open-source software.
  - Environmental Protection Agency (EPA) Environmental Dataset Gateway (EDG, https://edg.epa.gov/metadata/catalog/main/home.page).
  - USGS ScienceBase (https://www.sciencebase.gov/catalog/) is a dynamic query returning data assets with OPeNDAP end points.
  - U.S. Census TIGERweb (https://tigerweb.geo.census.gov/) is a Web-based system that offers visualization tools for geospatial information.
- WFS:
  - USGS ScienceBase (https://www.sciencebase.gov/catalog/) is a dynamic query returning data assets with OPeNDAP end points.
  - The USGS National Map (http://nationalmap.gov/) is a topographic information service.
- WMTS:
  - NASA Global Imagery Browse Services (GIBS, https://earthdata.nasa.gov/about-eosdis/science-system-description/eosdis-components/global-imagery-browse-services-gibs) is open source.

3.5 Testing Tool Programs

Several organizations, including OGC and the NSF-sponsored Long-Term Ecological Network (LTER), have developed various tools and services to support test implementations for the recommended standards. These are briefly described below.

- OGC Compliance Program (http://cite.opengeospatial.org/) offers tools and services for testing implementations.
- NSF Long-Term Ecological Research (LTER) Program (https://im.lternet.edu/projects/eml_congruency_checker) has developed a method of testing "metadata congruence" that could be extended to test how the data served by a service matches the description in the metadata.

3.6 Metrics

The following metrics will be measured automatically by gathering statistical information from authoritative data catalogs (e.g., data.gov, Geoplatform.gov).

- Percentage of metadata records or catalog entries with links to data-access services.

- Number of datasets that meet the U.S. Chief Information Officer qualifications for Open Data: publicly accessible under an open license with no restrictions on reuse. See the full Open Data Principles at https://project-open-data.cio.gov/principles.

- Relative popularity among data providers of each type of data-access service.

3.7 Known Limitations

Domain- or standard-specific limitations may be relevant to users. Typical limitations may include:

- Existing standards may need additional constraints, extensions, or profiles to provide more-consistent interoperability.

- Some types of biological data may not match any of the feature types listed above.

- Some types of social science/economics data may not match any of the feature types listed above.

- Different standards are needed for video or audio environmental observations (e.g., for undersea video).

4. Data Documentation

4.1 Introduction

Many scientific datasets and products are documented using approaches and tools developed by scientists and data collectors to support their own analysis and understanding. Such documentation exists in scientific papers, Web pages, user guides, and other *ad hoc* formats, each with associated storage and preservation strategies. This customized and often unstructured approach may be sufficient for independent investigators or individuals working in the confines of a particular laboratory or community, but makes the data difficult for users outside of these small groups to discover, access, use, and understand without consulting the data creators.

Metadata (the collected information describing data's structure and source) provides well-defined content in structured representations. When complete and accurate, metadata allows users to access and quickly understand many aspects of datasets regardless of their source. Metadata can also be integrated into discovery and analysis tools, and can provide consistent reference to external documentation.

Metadata standards provide element names, conventions, and associated structures that can describe a wide variety of digital resources. The definitions of these elements and accepted values are intended to be sufficiently broad to satisfy the metadata needs of various disciplines. These standards also include references to external documentation and well-defined mechanisms for adding structured information to address specific community needs.

The standards below, properly applied, can be used to meet the following DMP from the GEO Strategic Plan:

- **DMP-4**: Data will be comprehensively documented, including all elements necessary to access, use, understand, and process, preferably via formal structured metadata based on international or community-approved standards. To the extent possible, data will also be described in peer-reviewed publications referenced in the metadata record.

4.2 Standards and Protocols

The Common Framework recommends standard approaches for two types of metadata: dataset documentation (including information about the time period and area covered by the data, distribution methods, quality control, and points-of-contact for further information), and instrument specifications (detailed description of a sensor's characteristics).

4.2.1 Dataset Documentation

- **International metadata standard for geographic information ISO 19115-1**
  (http://www.iso.org/iso/home/store/catalog_tc/catalog_detail.htm?csnumber=53798)

  - **ISO 19115-3** defines the Extensible Markup Language (XML) encoding for 19115-1
    (http://standards.iso.org/iso/19115/-3/mdt/1.0/index.html).

  - **ISO 19157** is used for data-quality information
    (http://www.iso.org/iso/home/store/catalog_tc/catalog_detail.htm?csnumber=32575).

  - These are the newest versions of the ISO metadata standard. The older 19115-2 remains in wide use, but migration to the newer standard is encouraged whenever possible.

- o FGDC CSDGM is accepted for legacy datasets that cannot comply with the newer international metadata standards.

4.2.2 Instrument Specifications

- **SensorML** (http://www.opengeospatial.org/standards/sensorml) provides a robust and semantically tied means of defining processes and processing components associated with the measurement and post-measurement transformation of observations.

4.3 Methods and Practices

Support for Project Open Data metadata schema: for Earth Observations, preferred method is conversion from ISO XML (or other native format) to JavaScript Object Notation (JSON, *e.g.*, via XML stylesheet—XSLT).

4.4 Implementations

Several example implementations and the supporting standards are described below.

4.4.1 Software Available to Help Implement Standards

Two common open-source implementations for Earth observations are:

- ncISO is an open-source command-line utility for automating metadata analysis and ISO metadata generation for THREDDS (http://www.unidata.ucar.edu/software/thredds/current/tds/) catalog (http://www.ngdc.noaa.gov/eds/tds/).
- Apache Spatial Information System (http://sis.apache.org/) is an open-source geospatial toolkit, which provides an implementation of ISO 19115-2 and ISO 19139.

4.4.2 Examples of Implementation

Examples of implementation by government and non-profit organizations are:

- OpenTopography (http://www.opentopography.org/) is a USGS and NSF-supported catalog of topography data that uses the ISO 19115 metadata standard.
- NASA's Common Metadata Repository (https://earthdata.nasa.gov/about/science-system-description/eosdis-components/common-metadata-repository) provides mappings between metadata standards, including ISO 19115.

5. Compatible Formats and Vocabularies

5.1 Introduction

A major goal of the Common Framework is to bring about improved interoperability among the data assets coming from observation systems. This approach requires the ability to write software and applications that combine, integrate, and synthesize observations. Interoperability requires compatibility among data systems at the format level, at least in terms of data-exchange formats. Interoperability also requires compatibility in data models and vocabularies so that, for instance, precipitation data from one source can be compared to rainfall data from another source. This aspect of the Common Framework focuses on the underlying compatibility among Earth-observing data systems, translation mechanisms, common data models, vocabularies, and semantics.

A fundamental decision point in developing the Common Framework was the determination that all data systems complying with this framework must support spatiotemporal queries and constraints based on the Earth system. These queries could be either explicit, as in the case of an Earth-based coordinate reference system (or spatial reference system), or implicit, as in the case of a spatial framework such as hydrologic unit boundaries. For temporal constraints, parameters can be either explicit, based on standard encoding such as ISO8601 date/time variables, or implicit, such as geologic time periods. The space/time constraint or parameterization is assumed to be in place and available for discovering data, as in through catalog-service queries, and for accessing and using data, either through datasets being divided based on these parameters or through subsetting capabilities and available for use in various ways.

The standards below, applied properly, can be used to meet the following DMP from the GEO Strategic Plan:

- **DMP-3**: Data should be structured using encodings that are widely accepted in the target user community and aligned with organizational needs and observing methods, with preference given to non-proprietary international standards.

5.2 Standards and Protocols

Several standards and protocols for various types of data are included below. Additionally, certain supporting controlled vocabularies are described to encourage adoption and to promote interoperability.

5.2.1 Data Formats

For numerical data:

- NetCDF4/HDF5 (Network Common Data Form, http://www.unidata.ucar.edu/software/netcdf/) is the most recent version developed by Unidata. NetCDF4 uses HDF5 (Hierarchical Data Format, http://www.hdfgroup.org/HDF5/) as its storage layer.

For imagery:

- GeoTIFF (http://trac.osgeo.org/geotiff/) is a public-domain metadata standard that allows georeferencing information to be embedded within a Tagged Image File Format (TIFF) file.

For points/lines/polygons:

- Geography Markup Language (GML, http://www.opengeospatial.org/standards/gml) is the XML grammar defined by OGC to express geographical features. Use of GML sometimes requires specific profiles in particular areas, especially various kinds of *in situ* measurements. For example:

  - For hydrologic data, the Common Framework recommends WaterML2.0 (http://www.opengeospatial.org/standards/waterml).

  - For weather data, the Common Framework recommends Weather Information Exchange Model (WXXM, http://www.wxxm.aero/public/subsite_homepage/homepage.html).[6]

5.2.2 Controlled Vocabularies

Many communities of practice and research communities around specific domains have created controlled vocabularies to aid in ease of communication and proper reuse of data. It is strongly recommended to use relevant controlled vocabularies as much as possible.

Spatial Reference System: There are many different spatial reference systems in use, and data developers sometimes create their own for various purposes. The recommendation is to use:

- European Petroleum Survey Group (EPSG, http://www.epsg.org/) and Geodetic Parameter Dataset (http://www.epsg-registry.org/).

Hydrologic Units: Hydrography is important for many uses of Earth-observation data and is complex enough to require its own reference system. The recommendation is to use:

- National Hydrography Dataset (http://nhd.usgs.gov/) the Watershed Boundary Dataset, which is available as a service (http://services.nationalmap.gov/arcgis/rest/services/nhd/MapServer) and for download (ftp://rockyftp.cr.usgs.gov/vdelivery/Datasets/Staged/WBD/).

  - Keywords: Controlled lists of keywords for use in tagging data can aid in data search and discovery as well as with interoperability. The recommendation is to use:

- OMB Circular A-16, "Coordination of Geographic Information and Related Spatial Data Activities" (https://www.whitehouse.gov/omb/circulars_a016_rev/). Reissued in August 2002, OMB Circular A-16 establishes FGDC with its structure and responsibilities, and the appendices include definitions related to Geographic Information that are useful for universal adoption.

- NASA's Global Change Master Directory (GCMD, http://gcmd.nasa.gov/learn/keyword_list.html). GCMD is a lexicon of terms related to global-change research.

Parameter Names: For naming data parameters in metadata fields, the recommendation is to use:

- Climate Forecast Metadata Conventions Standard Names (http://cfconventions.org/standard-names.html).

---

[6] The USGEO Data Management Working Group is still assessing a potential consensus format for *in-situ* ocean data and intends to add a recommendation in a future published update of this document.

Content Models: The recommendation is to use:

- U.S. Geoscience Information Network (http://schemas.usgin.org/home/) provides "community" content models.

- Darwin Core (http://rs.tdwg.org/dwc/) provides biological-species observations.

- NEPAnode (http://nepanode.anl.gov/) provides open geospatial Web applications for collaborating on data, maps, and projects designed for non-GIS experts.

5.3 Methods and Practices

While having data in widely used formats is crucial, those formats can be used in ways that will not be compatible. It is important to test sufficiently to verify that content provided is readable by tools that users employ. It is recommended to validate file contents by using format and syntax checkers, if available.

5.4 Implementations

Building on the National Hydrography Dataset (NHD), USGS and EPA have collaborated on the production of the NHD Plus (http://www.horizon-systems.com/nhdplus/), which provides data down to the catchment level and is available via services from the EPA (http://water.epa.gov/scitech/datait/tools/waters/services/mapping_services.cfm) and downloads (http://www.horizon-systems.com/NHDPlus/V2NationalData.php) from Horizon Systems, a commercial partner in the NHD.

Appendix:
Related Policies

National Strategy for Civil Earth Observations

In April 2013, OSTP published the *National Strategy for Civil Earth Observations* (National Strategy), which promoted the importance of data management and delivery. The National Strategy laid out a set of principles that all agencies should use when managing Earth-observation data. These principles are:

- **Full and open access**: Earth observations should be fully and openly available to all users promptly, in a nondiscriminatory and platform-agnostic manner, and generally free of charge wherever possible. Agencies may set user charges consistent with OMB Circular A-130.

- **Preservation**: Earth observations should be managed as an asset and preserved for future use.

- **Information data quality**: Earth observations should be of known quality and fully documented.

- **Ease of use**: Earth observations should be easily discoverable, searchable, and accessible online using interoperable services and standardized, machine-readable formats that encourage the broadest possible use.

The National Strategy also explained the benefit of using data-management standards as follows:

> Standards are common rules, conditions, guidelines, or characteristics for data and related processes, technology, and organization. The broad use of a small set of common data, metadata, and protocol standards across Federal agencies (and international standards where possible) for data development, documentation, and exchange enhances the utility of Earth observations, decreases the cost of using the data, and helps Federal agencies avoid redundancies and waste.

> Different types of standards are applicable to various aspects of the data life cycle, including standards for data quality, metadata standards that specify the content and structure of documentation about a dataset, and interoperability standards that specify the content and structure of the digital data and how services will interact. The use of existing national and international data, metadata, and protocol standards is recommended. Because such standards are often general-purpose and require specialization for specific data types, agencies are encouraged to publish the conventions, profiles, and examples they adopt to make these standards more applicable to their data. Collaboration among and within agencies is encouraged to adopt common conventions for using existing standards to maximize compatibility.

This document is the outcome of a collaboration of many agencies involved in USGEO to recommend common practices, and thus addresses this recommendation of the *National Strategy*. The complete *National Strategy for Civil Earth Observations* can be found here:

https://www.whitehouse.gov/sites/default/files/microsites/ostp/nstc_2013_earthobsstrategy.pdf.

National Plan for Civil Earth Observations

In July 2014, the Office of Science and Technology Policy published the *National Plan for Civil Earth Observations*. The document listed several supporting actions that were required to meet the Plan's priorities. The second-highest-priority supporting action was to "improve data access, management, and interoperability." The Common Framework addresses many of the tasks that this action called upon agencies to undertake, including:

- Promote implementation of end-to-end life-cycle data management, including data-management principles, guidance, and data policy....

- Encourage the development and use of uniform methodologies and practices across Federal agencies for common services in the handling of Earth-observation data to increase interoperability through improved metadata standardization....

The complete *National Plan for Civil Earth Observations* can be found here:

https://www.whitehouse.gov/sites/default/files/microsites/ostp/NSTC/2014_national_plan_for_civil_earth_observations.pdf.

Big Earth Data Initiative

The Big Earth Data Initiative (BEDI) is a cross-agency activity supported by OSTP and OMB, and coordinated by the USGEO DMWG. Available BEDI funding is used to directly improve data from NASA, NOAA, and USGS, according to the recommendations of this Common Framework.

Guidance for BEDI comes from the April 2013 *National Strategy for Civil Earth Observations*, and is complementary to Executive Order 13642, "Making Open and Machine Readable the New Default for Government Information," and the associated OMB Memorandum M-13-13, "Open Data Policy— Managing Information as an Asset," both dated May 9, 2013. BEDI aims to improve the discovery, access, and use of all federally held Earth-system data with a high impact for public- and private-sector decision-making. Its objectives are to: (1) maximize the availability of data and information and ensure dissemination in a timely and usable manner; (2) facilitate the transformation of observations and data into useful information through the use of open, machine-readable formats and Application Programming Interfaces (APIs); (3) increase interoperability of Earth-system data and tools in order to encourage the development and use of tools and practices across Federal agencies; and (4) support the development of information products and tools that directly support decision-making.

Open Data Initiatives

Office of Science and Technology Policy Requirement for Agency Public Access Plans

In February 2013, OSTP Director John Holdren directed Federal agencies with more than $100 million per year in R&D expenditures to develop plans for increasing access to the results of federally funded research. Agency plans must ensure that researchers better account for and manage the digital data resulting from federally funded scientific research. Among the objectives for public access to scientific data are that agencies' plans should:

- Maximize access, by the general public and without charge, to digitally format scientific data created with Federal funds.

- Ensure the development and appropriate evaluation of data management plans describing proposed procedures for long-term preservation of, and access to, scientific data.

- Include mechanisms to ensure that intramural and extramural researchers comply with data-management plans and policies.

- Promote the deposit of data in publicly accessible databases, where appropriate and available.

- Develop approaches for identifying and providing appropriate attribution to scientific datasets that are made available under each agency's plan.

The full public-access memo can be found here:

http://www.whitehouse.gov/sites/default/files/microsites/ostp/ostp_public_access_memo_2013.pdf

Office of Management and Budget Open Data Policy

On May 9, 2013, President Obama issued Executive Order 13642, "Making Open and Machine Readable the New Default for Government Information." The Office of Management and Budget (OMB) amplified this order by issuing on the same day memorandum M-13-13 with the subject "Open Data Policy— Managing Information as an Asset." This memorandum said, in part:

> Specifically, this Memorandum requires agencies to collect or create information in a way that supports downstream information processing and dissemination activities. This includes using machine-readable and open formats, data standards, and common core and extensible metadata for all new information creation and collection efforts. It also includes agencies ensuring information stewardship through the use of open licenses and review of information for privacy, confidentiality, security, or other restrictions to release. Additionally, it involves agencies building or modernizing information systems in a way that maximizes interoperability and information accessibility, maintains internal and external data asset inventories, enhances information safeguards, and clarifies information management responsibilities."

The Executive Order can be found here:

https://www.whitehouse.gov/the-press-office/2013/05/09/executive-order-making-open-and-machine-readable-new-default-government-

The full OMB memorandum can be found at:

http://www.whitehouse.gov/sites/default/files/omb/memoranda/2013/m-13-13.pdf

Group on Earth Observations Data-Management Principles

In 2014, the international Group on Earth Observations (GEO) Data-Management Principles Task Force (DMP-TF) developed a set of principles intended to maximize the value and benefit of data shared through GEOSS. The following principles were adopted by GEO in 2015 as part of its Strategic Plan. The USGEO Common Framework directly supports Data-Management Principles #1, 2, 3, 4, and 10:

- Discoverability

  o **DMP-1**: Data and all associated metadata will be discoverable through catalogs and search engines, and data access and use conditions, including licenses, will be clearly indicated.

- Accessibility

  o **DMP-2**: Data will be accessible via online services, including, at minimum, direct download but preferably user-customizable services for visualization and computation.

- Usability

  o **DMP-3**: Data should be structured using encodings that are widely accepted in the target user community and aligned with organizational needs and observing methods, with preference given to non-proprietary international standards.

  o **DMP-4**: Data will be comprehensively documented, including all elements necessary to access, use, understand, and process, preferably via formal structured metadata based on international or community-approved standards. To the extent possible, data will also be described in publications referenced in the metadata record.

  o **DMP-5**: Data will include provenance metadata indicating the origin and processing history of raw observations and derived products, to ensure full traceability of the product chain.

- o **DMP-6**: Data will be quality-controlled and the results of quality control shall be indicated in metadata; data made available in advance of quality control will be flagged in metadata as unchecked.

- Preservation

  - o **DMP-7**: Data will be protected from loss and preserved for future use; preservation planning will be for the long term and include guidelines for loss prevention, retention schedules, and disposal or transfer procedures.

  - o **DMP-8**: Data and associated metadata held in data-management systems will be periodically verified to ensure integrity, authenticity and readability.

- Curation

  - o **DMP-9**: Data will be managed to perform corrections and updates in accordance with reviews, and to enable reprocessing as appropriate; where applicable this shall follow established and agreed procedures.

  - o **DMP-10**: Data will be assigned appropriate persistent, resolvable identifiers to enable documents to cite the data on which they are based and to enable data providers to receive acknowledgement of use of their data.

As a member of GEO, the U.S. Government supports the goal of full implementation of these principles.

Definitions and Descriptions

API—Application Programming Interface, a set of routines, protocols, and tools for building software applications, which expresses a software component in terms of its operations, inputs, outputs, and underlying types to allow automated access to machine-readable information.

BEDI—Big Earth Data Initiative, a cross-agency budget initiative aiming to improve Earth-observation data discoverability, accessibility, and usability.

Data—in this document, refers to Earth-observation data, meaning geo-referenced digital information about Earth, including the observations, metadata, imagery, derived products, data-processing algorithms (including computer source code and its documentation), and forecasts and analyses produced by computer models. Non-digital data, published papers, preserved geological or biological samples, or other media that have not been digitized are not included in this definition.

CENRS—Committee on Environment, Natural Resources, and Sustainability, part of the National Science and Technology Council.

DAP—Data Access Protocol, a data-transmission protocol designed specifically for science data relying on HTTP and Multipurpose Internet Mail Extensions standards.

DMP—Data-Management Principles, principles adopted by GEOSS to guide data stewardship.

DMWG—Data Management Working Group, a working group under the USGEO Subcommittee of the CENRS.

FGDC—Federal Geographic Data Committee, an interagency body within the U.S. Government that promotes coordinated development, use, sharing, and dissemination of geospatial data on a national basis.

GEO—Group on Earth Observations, an international intergovernmental body that coordinates Earth-observation and data systems for societal benefit.

GEOSS—Global Earth Observation System of Systems, a system being developed by GEO to deliver Earth-observation data to end users and decision makers.

HDF—Hierarchical Data Format, a suite of open-source technologies to support scientific data.

HTTP—Hypertext Transfer Protocol

ISO (International Organization for Standardization)—an independent, non-governmental membership organization that develops voluntary standards.

NetCDF—Network Common Data Form, a set of software libraries and self-describing, machine-independent data formats.

NSTC—National Science and Technology Council

OGC—Open Geospatial Consortium, an international industry consortium of companies, government agencies, and universities developing publicly available interface standards.

OPeNDAP—Open-source Project for a Network Data Access Protocol

URL—Uniform Resource Locator

USGEO—U.S. Group on Earth Observations, an interagency subcommittee of the CENRS which enables national-level coordination of Earth observations, data management, and related interagency and international activities.

WFS—Web Feature Service

WMS—Web Map Service

XML—Extensible Markup Language, a language that defines a set of rules for encoding documents in a format that is both human- and machine-readable.

www.ingramcontent.com/pod-product-compliance
Lightning Source LLC
Chambersburg PA
CBHW081138280526
45787CB00007B/3135